AF371464

This Cute Bear book belongs to

_ _ _ _ _ _ _ _ _

_ _ _ _ _ _ _ _ _

It was a wonderful summer day. The sun had just appeared,and its rays gently caressed the fluffy cheek of Benny Bear. He rubbed his sleepy eyes and opened them. As soon as he did, Benny remembered — today was his mum's birthday.

Yesterday, before going to bed, little Benny realized he had forgotten to pick out a present for his mum. He felt very sad and told himself that he would find the best one in the morning.

He quickly jumped out of bed, brushed his teeth, got dressed, and sneaked past the kitchen where his mum was preparing the most delicious honey cake. He went outside and hopped on his bike.

Benny was riding so fast towards his best friend's house —Bobo Beaver, that he almost hit a tree. When he reached the tiny house, Benny noticed that Bobo was working on something with his dad. As soon as Bobo saw Benny, he jumped up joyfully and ran to greet him.

'Hello, Benny! I'm glad you came', said Bobo. 'Do you want to help me? Dad and I are making a bed for me.'

'Hello, Bobo! I would love to help, but I have an important task. I need to quickly find the best present for mum. She's celebrating her birthday today.'

'Well then, let's look together,' Bobo suggested. 'You can help me with the bed later.'

'Good idea! But where should we start?' asked Benny.

'You know what?' said Bobo. 'Let's ask for advice from Grandpa Owl!
He really knows everything.'

And so, Benny and Bobo went to Grandpa Owl's place. When he saw them, the old owl smiled and said, 'Hello, children! What are you doing here so early?'

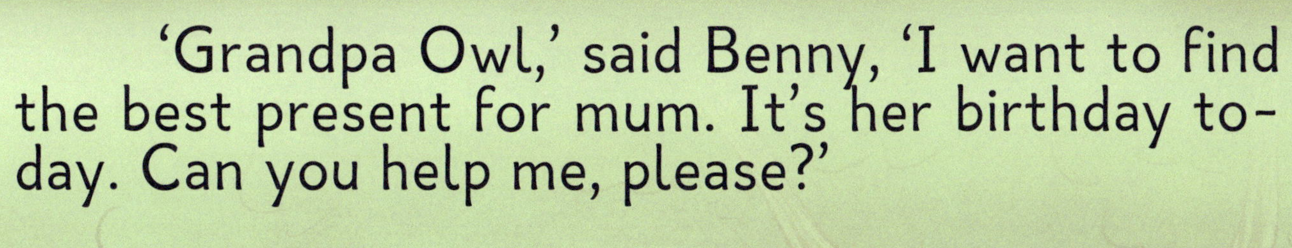

'Grandpa Owl,' said Benny, 'I want to find the best present for mum. It's her birthday to-day. Can you help me, please?'

'Oh, I see. Then it must be something very special. Think about what would make your mum happy most of all! What is that one thing that will make her the happiest?'

Benny pondered. Countless ideas swirled in his mind, but none seemed right. He felt sad.
'I don't know. I can't think of anything so special.'

'Hm, I suggest,' said Grandpa Owl, 'you go to the Quiet Lake. Stay there for a while and be silent. Then ask your heart. It knows best and will give you an answer.'

Benny thanked Grandpa Owl and Bobo and headed to the Quiet Lake. When he arrived, he sat in the meadow, closed his eyes, and said, 'Dear heart, you know best. What is the most beautiful present for mum?'

And then Benny saw how his mum's eyes sparkled when he hugged her, when he kissed her, when he gave her a little bouquet of fragrant forest flowers, and when he said I love you, mum!

Benny opened his eyes wide. He smiled, jumped up, and ran to the most beautiful forest glade with flowers. He gathered the most beautiful bouquet and, satisfied, headed home.

Mummy Bear had already prepared the delicious honey cake and was about to wake up her sleepy bear.

When she entered the bedroom, she saw that Benny wasn't there. She started looking for him.

She even went out into the garden to
check if he was playing. But Benny wasn't there.
At that moment, from the path, she heard...
'Mum, mummy, happy birthday! I love
you, mum!'

And he handed her the bouquet. She was so happy! She kissed him and said, 'I love you too, my dear little bear!'
Then they hugged and went to have some delicious cake.

Benny hadn't forgotten Bobo's and Grandpa Owl's help. He brought them some of mum's cake and helped Bobo put the bed together, because a friend in need is a friend indeed.

And so... when it's hard for you to make a decision, dear child, listen to your heart! It knows best.

FINISH
START

Find the 7 differences

Draw
Benny!

Happy Coloring!

Made in the USA
Monee, IL
07 July 2026